THE SAUSAGE IS A CUNNING BIRD . . .

With feathers long and wavy;
It swims about the frying pan
And makes its nest in gravy.

This playground song is just one of
many humorous poems and verses
within, guaranteed to entertain and
amuse you.

About the editors

Jennifer Curry gave up teaching so that she could write, and she is now the author of more than eleven plays and operettas, eighteen books, and innumerable newspaper and magazine articles. Recently she and Graeme Curry have established a successful and enjoyable working relationship – something fairly unusual for a mother and son to achieve. Despite their different tastes in poetry they like working as a team and have already produced several lively anthologies for children.

THE SAUSAGE IS
A CUNNING BIRD

Chosen by Jennifer
and Graeme Curry

Illustrated by Penny Simon

KNIGHT BOOKS
Hodder and Stoughton

For Tessa, with love

This collection copyright © Jennifer and Graeme Curry 1983
Illustrations copyright © Hodder & Stoughton Ltd 1983

British Library C.I.P.

Curry, Jennifer
  The sausage is a cunning bird.
  I. Title   II. Curry, Graeme
  823'.914[J]   PZ7

  ISBN 0 340 33204 2

---

*The characters and situations in this book are entirely
imaginary and bear no relation to any real person or
actual happening*

Printed and bound in Great Britain for Hodder and
Stoughton Paperbacks, a division of Hodder and
Stoughton Ltd., Mill Road, Dunton Green, Sevenoaks,
Kent (Editorial Office: 47 Bedford Square, London,
WC1 3DP) by Cox and Wyman Ltd, Reading.
Photoset by Rowland Phototypesetting Ltd.,
Bury St Edmunds, Suffolk

CONTENTS

Black Comedy

Story-Time

Acknowledgements   95

INTRODUCTION

One beautiful summer's day, Auntie Jo took the children down to the river for a picnic. After the meal she reached into the basket, took out a book of funny verse, and read them poems about fairies and bunnies. The children were itching to get on with their game of French cricket and to have some fun. However, they had a good laugh when Auntie Jo looked skyward and was sponned in the eye by a migrating swallow. And when, seconds later, a slimy black alligator emerged from the water and devoured Auntie Jo with one enormous gulp, their afternoon was complete.

These kids, far from being monstrous savages, are just like all the kids we know. So, lovers of fairies and bunnies, stop here. But if you're a bit silly, like weird and wonderful creatures, and feel slightly misunderstood by all those grown-ups who organise your life – then this is the book for you. Today, or tomorrow, pull on your jeans and go back to that river bank, not forgetting to take an umbrella and a stick to jam between the alligator's jaws. And take the book along as well. Because the one thing that Auntie Jo *did* get right, before her unfortunate accident, is that poems should be read aloud. Here you'll find funny sounds, nonsense, and games with words.

It's not easy to make a selection from all your

favourite funny poems. And it's even more difficult making your selection with someone else, because you have to explain to them why *their* favourites aren't half as funny as yours. But this is our choice. Some are by very famous poets, some by not very famous poets, and some by children who may be famous poets one day. They all make us laugh – and we hope that they will make you laugh too.
J. C. and G. C.

Stuff and Nonsense

A WISP OF A WASP

I'm a wisp of a wasp with a worry,
I'm hiding somewhere in Surrey
I've just bit upon
The fat sit upon
   of the King – so I left in a hurry.

Colin West

BEES

Every bee
that
ever was
was
partly
sting
and partly
. . . buzz.

 Jack Prelutsky

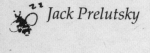

THE WISH

I wish I was a little grub
With whiskers round my tummy,
I'd climb into a honey-pot
And make my tummy gummy.

Anon

ONLY MY OPINION

Is a caterpillar ticklish?
  Well, it's always my belief
That he giggles, as he wiggles
  Across a hairy leaf.

Monica Shannon

A CENTIPEDE

A centipede was happy quite,
Until a frog in fun
Said, 'Pray, which leg comes after which?'
This raised her mind to such a pitch,
She lay distracted in the ditch
Considering how to run.

Anon

A LITTLE WORM

Today I saw a little worm
Wriggling on his belly.
Perhaps he'd like to come inside
And see what's on the Telly.

Spike Milligan

GRUESOME

I was sitting in the sitting room
toying with some toys
when from a door marked: 'GRUESOME'
There came a GRUESOME noise.

Cautiously I opened it
and there to my surprise
a little GRUE lay sitting
with tears in its eyes

'Oh little GRUE please tell me
what is it ails thee so?'
'Well I'm so small,' he sobbed,
'GRUESSES don't want to know'

'Exercises are the answer,
Each morning you must DO SOME'
He thanked me, smiled,
and do you know what?
The very next day he . . .

Roger McGough

BARNYARD FOWLS

The barnyard fowls which lay our eggs
Have pointed beaks and scaly legs,
But some which are considered freaks
Have pointed legs and scaly beaks.

Anon

THE CANARY

The Song of the Canaries
Never varies
And when they're moulting
They're pretty revolting.

Ogden Nash

WHO TO PET AND NOT TO

Go pet a kitten, pet a dog,
Go pet a worm for practice,
But don't go pet a porcupine –
You want to be a cactus?

X. J. Kennedy

I HAVE LOTSE OF MOODS

I have lotse of moods
wen I am in a bad
mood I un, rolle the toilet rolle
when I am in a good
mood I rolle up the toilet rolle

Robert Shiress Whitson (aged 6)

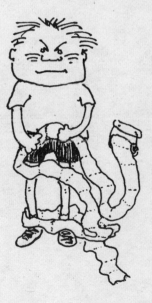

I WENT TO THE PICTURES TOMORROW

I went to the pictures tomorrow
I took a front seat at the back,
I fell from the pit to the gallery
And broke a front bone in my back.
A lady she gave me some chocolate,
I ate it and gave it her back.
I phoned for a taxi and walked it,
And that's why I never came back.

Anon

HARD, HARD, HARD

It's hard to lose a friend
When your heart is full of hope;
But it's worse to lose a towel
When your eyes are full of soap.

Anon

EXCUSE

I stayed up late last night
eating
breakfast
in order to save time in the morning
but when I woke up I was hungry again
and so
I was late
for school.

Bruce Garrard

SKINNY-MALINKY LONG-LEGS

Skinny-malinky long-legs,
   Umbrella feet,
Went tae the pictures
   And fell through the seat.
When the seat was mended
   He fell fast asleep,
Skinny-malinky long-legs,
   Umbrella feet.

Scottish Children's Rhyme

THE YOUNG BARD OF JAPAN

There was a young bard of Japan
Whose limericks never would scan.
When they asked why 'twas so,
He replied, 'Yes, I know,
But I make a rule of always trying to get just as
    many words into the last line as I possibly can.'

Anon

NOAH'S ARK

When Noah sailed the waters blue,
He had his troubles, same as you.
For forty days he drove his ark
Before he found a place to park.

Anon

'TIS MIDNIGHT

'Tis midnight, and the setting sun
Is slowly rising in the west;
The rapid rivers slowly run,
The frog is on his downy nest.
The pensive goat and sportive cow,
Hilarious, leap from bough to bough.

Anon

Peculiar People and Amiable Animals

MAGGIE

There was a young lady named Maggie,
Whose dog was enormous and shaggy;
The front end of him
Looked vicious and grim –
But the back end was friendly and waggy.

Anon

COUSIN REGGIE

Cousin Reggie
who adores the sea
lives in the Midlands
unfortunately.

He surfs down escalators
in department stores
and swims the High Street
on all of his fours.

Sunbathes on the pavement
paddles in the gutter
(I think our Reggie's
a bit of a nutter).

Roger McGough

LEARNER

Oh, Matilda, look at your Uncle Jim,
He's in the bathtub learning how to swim.
First he does the front stroke, then he does the side,
Now he's underwater, swimming against the tide.

Children's Rhyme

LEOPOLD ALCOCKS

Leopold Alcocks, my distant relation,
Came to my flat for a brief visitation.
He's been here since February, damn and blast him
My nerves and my furniture may not outlast him.

Leopold Alcocks is accident prone.
He's lost my bath plug, he's ruptured my
   telephone,
My antirrhinums, my motor bike, my sofa
There isn't anything he can't trip over.

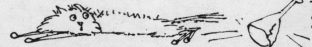

As he roams through my rooms, all my pussycats
   scatter.
My statuettes tremble, then plummet, then shatter.
My table lamps tumble with grim regularity.
My cut glass has crumbled and so has my charity.

Leopold Alcocks, an uncanny creature
He can't take tea without some misadventure:
He looks up from his tea cup with a smirk on his
   features
And a slice of my porcelain between his dentures.

He's upset my goldfish, he's jinxed my wisteria
My budgie's gone broody, my tortoise has hysteria.
He cleans my tea pots, my saucepans, with Brasso
And leaves chocolate finger prints on my Picasso.

Leopold Alcocks never known to fail
Working his way through my frail Chippendale.
One blow from his thighs (which are fearsomely
    strong)
Would easily fracture the wing of a swan.

Leopold Alcocks stirring my spleen
You are the grit in my life's vaseline.
A pox on you Alcocks! You've been here since
    Feb'ry
Go home and leave me alone with my debris.

So Leopold Alcocks, my distant relation
Has gone away home after his visitation.
I glimpsed him waving bye bye this last minute
Waving his hand with my door knob still in it.

Jake Thackray

FRED

Fred our friendly factory swan
filled with sliced bread and currant cake
floats low in the water he's sat upon
feeling majestic but with stomach ache

Quiet at night as if made of pewter
wishing for morning when he will be fed
happy to hear the start work hooter
unlike me who's still in bed

Philip Belton

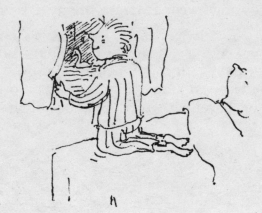

PLAYGROUND SONG

The sausage is a cunning bird
With feathers long and wavy;
It swims about the frying pan
And makes its nest in gravy.

Anon

DAME WIGGINS OF LEE

Dame Wiggins of Lee was a worthy old soul
As e'er threaded a needle, or washed in a bowl;
She held mice and rats in such antipathy,
That seven fine cats kept Dame Wiggins of Lee.

The rats and mice scared by this fierce-whiskered
    crew,
The seven poor cats soon had nothing to do;
So, as anyone idle she ne'er wished to see,
She sent them to school, did Dame Wiggins of Lee.

But soon she grew tired of living alone,
So she sent for her cats from school to come home:
Each rowing a wherry, returning, you see –
The frolic made merry Dame Wiggins of Lee.

To give them a treat she ran out for some rice;
When she came back they were skating on ice.
'I shall soon see one down. Aye, perhaps two or
    three,
I'll bet half-a-crown,' said Dame Wiggins of Lee.

While, to make a nice pudding, she went for a
    sparrow,
They were wheeling a sick lamb home in a barrow.
'You shall all have some sprats for your humanity,
My seven good cats,' said Dame Wiggins of Lee.

While she ran to the field, to look for its dam,
They were warming the bed for the poor sick lamb;
They turned up the clothes as neat as could be:
'I shall ne'er want a nurse,' cried Dame Wiggins of
  Lee.

She wished them goodnight, and went up to bed;
When lo! in the morning the cats were all fled.
But soon – what a fuss! 'Where can they all be?
Here, pussy, puss, puss!' cried Dame Wiggins of
  Lee.

The Dame's heart was nigh broke, so she sat down
  to weep,
When she saw them come back, each riding a
  sheep;
She fondled and patted each purring Tommy:
'Ah, welcome, my dears!' said Dame Wiggins of
  Lee.

The Dame was unable her pleasure to smother,
To see the sick lamb jump up to its mother.
In spite of the gout, and a pain in her knee,
She went dancing about, did Dame Wiggins of Lee.

Anon

DOWN BEHIND THE DUSTBIN

Down behind the dustbin
I met a dog called Sid.
He said he didn't know me,
But I'm pretty sure he did.

Down behind the dustbin
I met a dog called Jim.
He didn't know me
and I didn't know him.

Michael Rosen

THE HIPPOPOTAMUS

Consider the poor hippopotamus:
His life is unduly monotonous.
He lives half asleep
At the edge of the deep,
And his face is as big as his bottom is.

Anon

COWS

Half the time they munched the grass, and all the
  time they lay
Down in the water-meadows, the lazy month of
  May,
    A-chewing,
    A-mooing,
  To pass the hours away.

    'Nice weather,' said the brown cow.
    'Ah,' said the white.
    'Grass is very tasty.'
    'Grass is all right.'

Half the time they munched the grass, and all the
  time they lay
Down in the water-meadows, the lazy month of
  May,
    A-chewing,
    A-mooing,
  To pass the hours away.

    'Rain coming,' said the brown cow.
    'Ah,' said the white.
    'Flies is very tiresome.'
    'Flies bite.'

Half the time they munched the grass, and all the
   time they lay
Down in the water-meadows, the lazy month of
   May,
      A-chewing,
      A-mooing,
   To pass the hours away.

      'Time to go,' said the brown cow.
      'Ah,' said the white.
      'Nice chat.' 'Very pleasant.'
      'Night.' 'Night.'

Half the time they munched the grass, and all the
   time they lay
Down in the water-meadows, the lazy month of
   May,
      A-chewing,
      A-mooing,
   To pass the hours away.

James Reeves

THE FOUR FRIENDS

Ernest was an elephant, a great big fellow,
    Leonard was a lion with a six-foot tail,
George was a goat, and his beard was yellow,
    And James was a very small snail.

Leonard has a stall, and a great big strong one,
    Ernest had a manger, and its walls were thick,
George found a pen, but I think it was the
    wrong one,
    And James sat down on a brick.

Ernest started trumpeting, and cracked his
    manger,
    Leonard started roaring, and shivered his stall,
James gave the huffle of a snail in danger
    And nobody heard him at all.

Ernest started trumpeting and raised such a
    rumpus,
    Leonard started roaring and trying to kick,
James went a journey with the goat's new compass
    And he reached the end of his brick.

Ernest was an elephant and very well-intentioned,
    Leonard was a lion with a brave new tail,
George was a goat, as I think I have mentioned,
    But James was only a snail.

A. A. Milne

THE AARDVARK

The aardvark knows a lot of things,
but seldom has been heard
to say a single syllable
much less an aardvark word.

The aardvark surely would enjoy
the chance to make a sound,
but no one pays attention
when the aardvark comes around.

To so ignore the aardvark
makes the aardvark disinclined
to join in conversation
and reveal what's on his mind.

Jack Prelutsky

I'M NOT FRIGHTENED

I'm not frightened of Pussy Cats,
They only eat up mice and rats,
   But a Hippopotamus
    Could eat the Lotofus.

Spike Milligan

ODE TO A GOLDFISH

O
Wet
Pet!

Gyles Brandreth

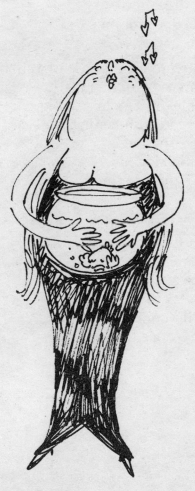

THE SONG OF THE CAMEL

'Canary-birds feed on sugar and seed,
    Parrots have crackers to crunch;
And, as for the poodles, they tell me the noodles
    Have chickens and cream for their lunch.
        But there's never a question
        About MY digestion –
        ANYTHING does for me!

'Cats, you're aware, can repose in a chair,
    Chickens can roost upon rails;
Puppies are able to sleep in a stable,
    And oysters can slumber in pails.
        But no one supposes
        A poor Camel dozes –
        ANY PLACE does for me!

'Lambs are inclosed where it's never exposed,
    Coops are constructed for hens;
Kittens are treated to houses well heated,
    And pigs are protected by pens.
        But a Camel comes handy
        Wherever it's sandy –
        ANYWHERE does for me!

'People would laugh if you rode a giraffe,
  Or mounted the back of an ox;
It's nobody's habit to ride on a rabbit,
  Or try to bestraddle a fox.
    But as for a Camel, he's
    Ridden by families –
  ANY LOAD does for me!

'A snake is as round as a hole in the ground,
  And weasels are wavy and sleek;
And no alligator could ever be straighter
  Than lizards that live in a creek.
    But a Camel's all lumpy
    And bumpy and humpy –
  ANY SHAPE does for me!'

Charles Edward Carryl

Word Games

LIFE IS BUTTER

Life is butter, life is butter;
Melancholy flower, melancholy flower;
Life is but a melon, life is but a melon;
Cauliflower, cauliflower.

Anon

DEAR EAGLE

'Dear Eagle' said Miss Macalary,
'Whilst I live in auld Tipperary
    You live in an eyrie',
    The Eagle said, 'Dearie,
I'd sooner live eyrie than therie.'

Eric Sykes

AN EGGSTRAVAGANCE

The Reverend Henry Ward Beecher
Called a hen 'a most elegant creature'.
   The hen, pleased with that,
   Laid two eggs in his hat,
And thus did the hen reward Beecher.

Oliver Wendell Holmes

RABBIT RACED A TURTLE

A rabbit raced a turtle,
You know the turtle won;
And Mister Bunny came in late,
A little hot cross bun!

Anon

I'LL BE DARNED

Said the toe to the sock,
   'Let me through, let me through!'
Said the sock to the toe,
   'I'll be darned if I do.'

Anon

BIGTROUSERS DAN

In the land of Rumplydoodle
where men eat jollips for tea,
and the cows in the hay
feel sleepy all day,
there's a wonderful sight to see.
On the banks of the River Bongbong,
in a hut made of turnips and cream,
sits a whiskery man,
name of Bigtrousers Dan,
and he plays with his brand new machine.
There are gronfles
and nogglets
and pluffles
and valves that go
ker-pling and ker-plang,
and a big sugar wheel
that revolves with a squeal
'till it's oiled with a chocolate meringue.
There are wurdlics
and flumdings
and crumchies
that go round just as fast as they can,
and a big chocolate ball
that makes no sound at all,
thanks to clever old
Bigtrousers Dan.

Peter Mortimer

W

The King sent for his wise men all
   To find a rhyme for W.
When they had thought a good long time
But could not think of a single rhyme,
   'I'm sorry,' said he, 'to trouble you.'

James Reeves

A WOMAN
TO HER SON DID UTTER

A woman to her son did utter
Go, my son, and shut the shutter.
The shutter's shut, the son did utter,
I cannot shut it any shutter.

Anon

EPITAPH ON A MARF

Wot a marf 'e'd got,
Wot a marf.
When 'e was a kid,
Goo' Lor' luv'll
'Is pore old muvver
Must 'a' fed 'im wiv a shuvvle.

Wot a gap 'e'd got,
Pore Chap,
'E'd never been known to larf,
Cos if 'e did
It's a penny to a quid
'E'd 'a' split 'is fice in 'arf.

Anon

ETHEL READ A BOOK

Ethel read,
Ethel read,
Ethel read a book.
Ethel read a book in bed,
She read a book on Ethelred.
The book that Ethel read in bed,
(The book on Ethelred) was red.
The book was red that Ethel read,
In bed on Ethelred.

Colin West

PHOEBE

A certain young chap named Bill Beebee
Was in love with a lady named Phoebe.
  'But,' said he, 'I must see
  What the licence fee be
Before Phoebe be Phoebe B. Beebee.'

Anon

THE NEW GNU

There was a sightseer named Sue,
Who saw a strange beast at the zoo.
   When she asked, 'Is it old?'
   She was smilingly told,
'It's not an old beast, but a gnu.'

Anon

NO HORSE COULD BE FOUND

A major, with wonderful force,
Called out in Hyde Park for a horse.
   All the flowers looked round,
   But no horse could be found,
So he just rhododendron, of course.

Anon

POP BOTTLES

Pop bottles pop-bottles in pop shops.
The pop-bottles Pop bottles poor Pop drops.
When Pop drops pop-bottles, pop-bottles plop.
When pop-bottles topple, Pop mops slop.

Anon

LAST NIGHT

The Eskimo sleeps on his white bearskin,
And sleeps rather well, I'm told.
Last night I slept in my little bare skin,
And caught a terrible cold.

Anon

Black Comedy

AN ACCIDENT HAPPENED
TO MY BROTHER JIM

An accident happened to my brother Jim
When somebody threw a tomato at him –
Tomatoes are juicy and don't hurt the skin,
But this one was specially packed in a tin.

Anon

THE BULB

I am a bulb,
Not a plant bulb,
but a light bulb,
'cos plant bulbs
are dim bulbs,
and I am a bright bulb.
Bugses eat plant bulbs
but I am a light bulb.
So I am invincibulb
except that I'm smashabulb,
CRASH

I *was* a live bulb,
but now I'm a dead bulb.

Helen Cooper (aged 13)

THE RABBIT'S
CHRISTMAS CAROL

I'm sick as a parrot,
I've lost me carrot,
I couldn't care less if it's
Christmas Day.

I'm sick as a parrot,
I've lost me carrot,
So get us a lettuce
Or . . . go away!

Kit Wright

ONE DAY AT
PERRANPORTH PET-SHOP

One day at Perranporth pet-shop
On a rather wild morning in June,
A lady from Par bought a budgerigar
And she sang to a curious tune:
'Say that you love me, my sweetheart,
My darling, my dovey, my pride,
My very own jewel, my dear one!'
'Oh lumme,' the budgie replied.

'I'll feed you entirely on cream-cakes
And doughnuts all smothered in jam,
And puddings and pies of incredible size,
And peaches and melons and ham.
And you shall drink whiskies and sodas,
For comfort your cage shall be framed.
You shall sleep in a bed lined with satin.'
'Oh crikey!' the budgie exclaimed.

But the lady appeared not to hear him
For she showed neither sorrow nor rage,
As with common-sense tardy and action foolhardy
She opened the door of his cage.
'Come perch on my finger, my honey,
To show you are mine, O my sweet.' –
Whereupon the poor fowl with a shriek and a howl
Took off like a jet down the street.

And he flew up above Cornwall
To ensure his escape was no failure,
Then his speed he increased and he flew south
    and east
To his ancestral home in Australia.
For although to the Australian abo
The word 'budgerigar' means 'good food',
He said, 'I declare I'll feel much safer there
Than in Bodmin or Bugle or Bude.'

Envoy
And I'm sure with the budgie's conclusion
You all will agree without fail:
Best eat frugal and free in a far-distant tree
Than down all the wrong diet in jail.

Charles Causley

THE SNAIL CAULD DICK
WHO WASENT IN VERY
GOOD NICK

There once was a snail cauld Dick
Who wasent in very good nick.
He would eat any thing he could find.
One day when Dick was laying in the sun
A big bird came along
    and got Dick by his shell.
Dick said to his self if I was in good nick
I might of got out of this Birds mouth
Before you can say Edward Heath.

Clare Ann Maller (aged 10)

ON NEVSKI BRIDGE

On Nevski Bridge a Russian stood
Chewing his beard for lack of food.
Said he, 'It's tough this stuff to eat
But a darn sight better than shredded wheat!'

Anon

HOW TO SCARE YOUR PARENTS

Bang your head upon your knee
Hang yourself upon a tree
Pull your legs out of their sockets
Now put fire works in your pockets
Go upstairs and go to bed
And make believe that you are dead

Thomas Joseph Divine (aged 8)

THE PARENT

Children aren't happy with nothing to ignore,
And that's what parents were created for.

Ogden Nash

A YOUNG LADY
NAMED ROSE

There was a young lady named Rose,
Who had a huge wart on her nose.
   When she had it removed,
   Her appearance improved,
But her glasses slipped down to her toes.

Anon

BETTY AT THE PARTY

'When I was at the party,'
   Said Betty, aged just four,
'A little girl fell off her chair
   Right down upon the floor.
And all the other little girls
   Began to laugh, but me –
I didn't laugh a single bit,'
   Said Betty seriously.

'Why not?' her mother asked her,
   Full of delight to find
That Betty – bless her little heart! –
   Had been so sweet and kind.
'Why didn't you laugh, my darling?
   Or don't you like to tell?'
'I didn't laugh,' said Betty,
   'Cause I'm the one who fell.'

Anon

GROWING

The sleeves of this jersey
Grow longer and longer:
They soon will stretch down to
My knee,

And though I'm becoming both
Taller and stronger
They grow so much faster
Than me

That unless very soon I get
Wider and fatter
It's perfectly simple
To see

I shall have to make do with no
Hands, thumbs or fingers
And NEVER take lumps
In my tea.

Jean Kenward

A LITTLE GIRL I HATE

I saw a little girl I hate
And kicked her with my toes.
She turned
And smiled
And KISSED me!
Then she punched me in the nose.

Arnold Spilka

CHESTER'S UNDOING

Chester Lester Kirkenby Dale
Caught his sweater on a nail.
As Chester Lester started to travel
So his sweater began to unravel.
A great long trail of crinkly wool
Followed Chester down to school.
Then his ears unravelled!
His neck and his nose!
Chester undid from his head
To his toes.
Chester's undone, one un-purl, two un-plain,
Who's got the pattern to knit him again?

Julie Holder

IF YOU SHOULD MEET A CROCODILE

If you should meet a crocodile,
Don't take a stick and poke him;
Ignore the welcome in his smile,
Be careful not to stroke him.

For as he sleeps upon the Nile,
He thinner gets and thinner;
And whene'er you meet a crocodile
He's ready for his dinner.

Anon

THE VISITOR

it came today to visit
and moved into the house
it was smaller than an elephant
but larger than a mouse

first it slapped my sister
then it kicked my dad
then it pushed my mother
oh! that really made me mad

it went and tickled rover
and terrified the cat
it sliced apart my necktie
and rudely crushed my hat

it smeared my head with honey
and filled the tub with rocks
and when i yelled in anger
it stole my shoes and socks

that's just the way it happened
it happened all today
before it bowed politely
and softly went away

Jack Prelutsky

Story-Time

WE HEARD A POET TODAY

We heard a poet today.
He read some of his poems.
They weren't bad.
They were OK.
They were quite good really.
They were marvellous!

(I wish he'd stop looking over my shoulder.)

Anon

DAD KNOWS BEST!

Most parents like their holidays to be a cosy rest,
They think a nice relaxing place, with sunshine, is
   best.
But my Dad is quite different, he's very energetic
And holidays we spend with him, are bound to be
   athletic.

We've clambered up Ben Nevis, and we've
   tramped across the moors,
When many times we've wished, we could have
   stayed behind, indoors.
Last year we made a protest; said we'd stretch out
   in the sun,
And Dad must like it or lump it – that was our idea
   of fun!

I think he was surprised, because he just stood
   there and mumbled.
As we reached the Grand Hotel, he never even
   grumbled.
He sat down on the beach with us, and gazed right
   out to sea,
Spread suntan oil upon our backs as calmly as can
   be.

At first we were delighted, as we lay there in the
   sand.
With everything, we thought, conveniently at hand.

But after three whole days, that small suspicion gnawed
And finally, we realised the truth – that we were bored!

Mum began to fidget, she put aside her knitting,
My sister sighed and scowled a lot, I knew their teeth were gritting.
We didn't dare complain, for what we wanted most, we had,
Yet, happy as a sandboy in the sunshine lay our Dad!

Then my Dad began to smile – the smile became a grin,
'Why don't you all admit you're bored,' he said, 'it's not a sin!
I went out for a walk last night, and found a riding stable,
We'll spend the next week trekking, if you all feel fit and able!'

Now we've learnt that holidays without much kind of action
Cannot give us what we need, in terms of satisfaction.
Dad's ideas may cause us all to grumble or to joke,
But deckchairs on the beach can stay there, for other folk!

Christine Ann Farrell

WHEN I WAS YOUNG

When I was young, I didn't shout
Or throw my sister's dolls about.
I was a most delightful boy,
An everlasting parents' joy.
Well; not infrequently.

I didn't climb the apple tree
And bawl for Mum to rescue me,
Nor idly throw rough half-brick bats
Or persecute poor pussy cats.
Well; hardly frequently.

I was a most exemplary child.
I never sent my parents wild.
I always did as I was told,
I really was as good as gold.
Well; yes quite frequently.

When other boys scrumped from the tree
Those apples green, no-one saw me.
I never sneaked the strawberry jam
Or went motor-racing with the pram.
Well; just infrequently.

Would I knock conkers down with stones?
With risk to other children's bones?
Would I break down the garden fence?
Or worm my way through circus tents?
Oh; most infrequently.

A little paragon was I,
The apple of dear Granny's eye.
I must have been the noblest child
Yet somehow got my parents riled.
They beat me.
                    Frequently.

Robert Sparrow

WHEN I GROW UP

The books I read tell me
That what I want to be
When I grow up is
An engine driver
Or a footballer
Or Prime Minister.

But

An engine driver has
Unsociable hours, time in Scotland,
Solitude, a silly cap and a
Complaining British public,

A footballer has
Unsociable hours, early retirement,
Television interviewers, winter mud and a
Complaining British public,

A Prime Minister has
Unsociable hours, rather loud colleagues,
A grubby house in a London backstreet and a
Complaining British public.

So when I grow up
I shall be a clerk and
As I while away
My sociable hours I shall be
A bit of an engine driver,
A bit of a footballer,
A bit of a Prime Minister and a member of the
Complaining British public.

Benjamin Bolt

SUPERMARKET

I'm
lost
among a
maze of cans
behind a pyramid
of jams, quite near
asparagus and rice,
close to the Oriental spice,
and just before sardines.
I hear my mother calling, 'Joe.
Where are you, Joe?
Where did you
Go?' And I reply in a voice concealed among
the candied orange peel, and packs of Chocolate
Dreams.

'I
hear
you, Mother
dear, I'm here –
quite near the ginger ale
and beer, and lost among a
maze
of cans
behind a
pyramid of jams
quite near asparagus
and rice, close to the
Oriental spice, and just before sardines.'

But
still
my mother
calls me, 'Joe!
Where are you, Joe?
Where did you go?

'Somewhere
around asparagus
that's in a sort of
broken glass,
beside a kind of m-
ess-
y jell
that's near a tower of cans that
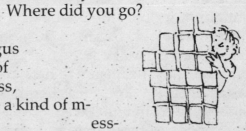
f
e
l
l

and squashed the Chocolate Dreams.

Felice Holman

AUNT KATE: A MORAL STORY

When Aunt Kate woke each shining day
She started nagging right away.
'Shut the window,' 'Open the door,'
'Pick your pyjamas up from the floor,'
'Let the cat in,' 'Make some tea,'
'Why do you never listen to me?'
'Stop fidgeting,' 'Your tie is bent.'
She started so and on it went
From breakfast through to supper-time,
Till even breathing seemed a crime.
Her nephews and her nieces too
Were at their wits' ends what to do.

One summer-time she made a plan
To spend a week with Cousin Anne.
She turned the gas off, packed her case,
Left her instructions all over the place.
She went to the station to catch her train,
And her nieces began to smile again.
Her nephews started to laugh and sing
And they wouldn't be quiet for anything.
Meanwhile at the station, Aunt Kate found
A way to boss everyone around;
Station master and guards and all
Were running about at her beck and call.
She complained of the service, the dirt and the
  crowd,
The trains were too dusty, their engines too loud.

Managers, Unions, Heads of the State
Could cope with the Press, but not with Aunt Kate.
They promised her Jaguars, planes or a bike
To avert the threat of a General Strike.
But she being averse to both pedals and flights
Stood with her ticket demanding her rights,
Until they came up with a masterful plan
For delivering Auntie to her Cousin Anne,

'If you'll drive the train it will all be all right,
The engine so quiet not a mouse could take fright.'
So Kate drove that diesel and felt her real power,
And she sang and she whistled for one happy
    hour.
Her hat had blown off, and her face and her hair
Were covered in oil, but she didn't care;
And Anne when she saw her just couldn't guess
That this jolly lady, in such a great mess,
Was querulous Kate whom she'd dreaded to meet.

All you British Aunties, too painfully neat,
Learn from this solemn and serious tale,
How you too can be changed if you'll travel by rail.

Shirley Toulson

BABIES ARE BORING

Babies are boring
(Oh yes they are!)
Don't believe mothers
or a doting papa.
Babies are boring,
their hands and their bellies,
their pink puffy faces
which wobble like jellies.
Accountants and grandmas
and sailors from Chile
when faced with a baby
act extraordinarily silly.
They grimace and they giggle,
say 'diddle-dum-doo',
they waggle their fingers
(stick their tongues out too).

They slaver and slurp
then they tickle its tummy
they gurgle and drool:
'Oh, he's just like his mummy!'
'Oh, his mouth is like Herbert's!'
'He's got Uncle Fred's nose!'
'My word, he looks healthy!'
'It's his feed, I suppose?'
Save me from baldness
and the old smell of kippers,
but most of all save me
from all gooey nippers.
I'm a brute, I'm a fiend
and no use to implore me
to tickle its chin,
because all babies bore me.

Peter Mortimer

FATHER SAYS

Father says
Never
let
me
see
you
doing
that
again
father says
tell you once
tell you a thousand times
come hell or high water
his finger drills my shoulder
never let me see you doing that again

My brother knows all his phrases off by heart
so we practise them in bed at night.

Michael Rosen

THE OUTLAW

Into the house of a Mrs MacGruder
Came a very big outlaw
With a real six-shooter,
And he kicked the door
With his cowboy boot
And he searched the place
For valuable loot,
And he didn't take off his cowboy hat
But he quickly unlimbered his cowboy gat
And he cocked the gun
And he took his aim
And he called that Mrs MacG by name
And he said in a terrible outlaw drawl,
'Git me that cake . . . and git it all!'

And Mrs MacGruder patted his head,
'You may have a slice with some milk,' she said.

Felice Holman

REFLECTION ON BABIES

A bit of talcum
Is always walcum.

Ogden Nash

Acknowledgements

The authors and publishers gratefully acknowledge permission to reprint copyright material to the following:
Dobson Books Ltd for 'A Wisp of a Wasp' from *Out of the Blue from Nowhere* and 'Ethel Read a Book' from *Back to Front and Back Again* by Colin West. Greenwillow Books (a division of William Morrow & Company) for 'Bees' and 'Aardvark' from *Zoo Doings* by Jack Prelutsky; copyright © 1970, 1983 by Jack Prelutsky. Also for 'The Visitor' from *The Queen of Eene* by Jack Prelutsky; copyright © 1970, 1978. Doubleday and Company, Inc. for 'Only My Opinion' from *Goose Grass Rhymes* by Monica Shannon; copyright 1930 by Doubleday and Company, Inc. Spike Milligan for 'A Little Worm' and 'I'm Not Frightened' from *Silly Verse for Kids*, published by Dobson Books Ltd. A. D. Peters and Co Ltd for 'Gruesome' by Roger McGough from *You Tell Me*, published by Kestrel Books Ltd. Curtis Brown Ltd; London, on behalf of the Estate of Ogden Nash for 'The Canary', 'The Parent' and 'Reflection on Babies' from *The Family Reunion* by Ogden Nash; also Little Brown and Company for 'The Canary', copyright 1940 by the Curtis Publishing Company (first appeared in the *Saturday Evening Post*), 'The Parent' copyright 1933 by Ogden Nash, 'Reflection on Babies', copyright 1940 by Ogden Nash – all from *Many Long Years Ago* by Ogden Nash. Associated Book Publishers Ltd for 'Who to Pet and Not To' by X. J. Kennedy from *Allsorts 7*; 'Cousin Reggie' by Roger McGough from *Sporting Relations*; 'The Four Friends' from *When We Were Very Young* by A. A. Milne, and 'Aunt Kate: a Moral Story' by Shirley Toulson from *Allsorts 6*, all published by Methuen London. Daily Mirror Children's Literary Competition 1975/76 for 'I Have Lotse of Moods' by Robert Shiress Whitson, 'How to Scare Your Parents' by Thomas J. Divine and 'Dad Knows Best' by Christine Ann Farrell. Bruce Garrard for 'Excuse'. W. H. Allen for 'Leopold Alcocks' by Jake Thackray from *Jake's Progress*. Philip Belton for 'Fred'. André Deutsch Ltd and Michael Rosen for 'Down Behind the Dustbin' from *Wouldn't You Like to Know* and 'Father Says' from *Mind Your Own Business*. Oxford University Press for 'Cows' and 'W' from *The Blackbird in the*

Lilac by James Reeves (1952). Gyles Brandreth for 'Ode to a Goldfish', originally published in *A Second Poetry Book* compiled by John Foster for Oxford University Press. Michael Joseph Ltd for 'Dear Eagle' by Eric Sykes, from *Milligan's Ark* by Spike Milligan, published by Michael Joseph with Jack Hobbs. Peter Mortimer for 'Bigtrousers Dan' and 'Babies are Boring', first published in *Utter Nonsense* (Iron Press, 1977) illustrated by Geoff Laws. W. H. Smith Children's Literary Competition 1978 for 'The Bulb' by Helen Cooper and 'The Snail Cauld Dick Who Wasent in Very Good Nick' by Clare Ann Maller. Jean Kenward for 'Growing'. David Higham Associates Ltd for 'One Day at Perranporth Pet-Shop by Charles Causley from *Figgie Hobbin*, published by Macmillan. 'A Little Girl I Hate' by Arnold Spilka originally appeared in *A Rumbudan of Nonsense*. Julie Holder for 'Chester's Undoing', originally published in *A Second Poetry Book* compiled by John Foster, published by Oxford University Press. Robert Sparrow for 'When I Was Young'. Kit Wright and Penguin Books Ltd for 'The Rabbit's Christmas Carol' from *Hot Dog and Other Poems* by Kit Wright. 'We Heard a Poet Today' originally appeared in *A Visit From a Poet*. Charles Scribner's Sons for 'The Outlaw' and 'Supermarket' by Felice Holman published in *At the Top of My Voice and Other Poems*, copyright © 1970 Felice Holman. Graeme Curry for 'When I Grow Up' by Benjamin Bolt.

The publishers have made every effort to trace copyright holders. If we have inadvertently omitted to acknowledge anyone we should be most grateful if this would be brought to our attention for correction at the first opportunity.